Mental Health:
The Ultimate Guide to Achieve Mental Toughness and Take Care of Yourself Without Seeing a Therapist

Casey Averson

Copyright © 2019 Casey Averson

All rights reserved.

ISBN-13: 9-781-7942-4475-7

CONTENTS

	Introduction	i
1	Chapter 1: What is Mental Health?	1
2	Chapter 2: Nutrition: How to Eat Smart for a Healthier Brain	11
3	Chapter 3: What Are the Mental Health Benefits of Exercise?	23
4	Chapter 4: How Gratitude Can Improve Your Mental Health	32
5	Chapter 5: Why Is Sleep so Crucial for Your Brain Health?	37
6	Chapter 6: How to Fight Anxiety and Depression Without Medication	44
7	Chapter 7: How to Reduce Stress with Mindfulness Meditation	53
8	Chapter 8: Why Is Self-Regulation so Important?	62
9	Chapter 9: Mental Health: Awareness Is Great, but Action Is Essential	72
10	Conclusion	87

Introduction

Congratulations on downloading *Mental Health: The Ultimate Guide to Achieve Mental Toughness and Take Care of Yourself Without Seeing a Therapist* and thank you for doing so. Mental health issues can affect anyone, regardless of how in control of their day to day lives they may seem. In fact, the type of mental health issue that you are dealing with isn't nearly as important as how you decide to deal with it once and for all

The following chapters will discuss a variety of ways for you to do just that, starting with a look at the concept of mental health as a whole as well as why it is so important to remain vigilant regarding your own. Next, you will learn all about the many ways that nutrition plays into mental health and how following the keto diet can leave your brain happy and healthy. To go along with a healthier diet, you will then learn about the many ways exercise can improve your mental health and a starter exercise plan that can help you get off the couch for good.

From there, you will learn how to develop an attitude of gratitude, as well as why doing so will leave your mental health in tip-top shape. Next, you will find information on why sleep is so vital for brain health, along with tips to help you improve your sleep once and for all. You will then find a discussion of cognitive behavioral therapy and how it can help you to fight depression and anxiety without medication successfully. The mental wellness tips continue from there as you learn all about the many ways mindfulness meditation helps to reduce stress as well as how to get started for yourself. Finally, you will find great tips for keeping things up in the long-term with self-regulation and other tips to ensure you take action when it comes to promoting your mental health.

There are plenty of books on this subject on the market, thanks again for choosing this one! Every effort was made to ensure that it is full of as much useful information as possible; please enjoy!

CHAPTER 1: WHAT IS MENTAL HEALTH?

Just as physical fitness helps the body to stay strong, mental fitness helps to achieve and sustain a state of good mental health. When a person is mentally healthy, they enjoy their life and environment, as well as the people in it. They find it easier to be creative, learn, try new things, and take risks. They are better able to cope with difficult times in their personal and professional lives as well. They still feel an expected amount of sadness and anger that can come with the death of a loved one, a job loss or relationship problems and other difficult events but, in time, they are able to get on with it and enjoy their lives once again.

Nurturing your mental health can also help to combat or prevent the mental health problems that are sometimes associated with a chronic physical illness. In some cases, it can prevent the onset or relapse of a physical or mental illness. Managing stress well, for instance, can have a positive impact on heart disease.

Chances are, you are already taking steps to sustain your mental health, as well as your physical health – you just might not realize it.

Mental health includes a person's social, psychological and emotional well-being as well as how they act feel and think.

Furthermore, it helps determine things such as how a person relates to others and the types of choices they might make when push comes to shove. No matter what age you are, your mental health is extremely important to your overall wellbeing. If you experience mental health issues, you may find that your behavior, mood and thought patterns could all be affected. Three of the main factors that contribute to mental health problems include:

- Biological factors, such as genes or brain chemistry
- Life experiences, such as trauma or abuse
- A family history of mental health problems

Lowers medical costs: One of the most significant benefits of regularly keeping up with your mental health is that you will likely pay less in medical costs on average. In fact, one study on anxiety disorders even showed that those with the disorder saw a decrease in doctor visits of 90 percent once they successfully completed a round of CBT treatment. More importantly for some, the preventative treatment ended up costing about 35 percent less in the short-term than treating the symptoms that letting the condition remain untreated in the long-term.

Additional studies have shown that those who allow their mental health issues to go untreated typically visit the doctor about twice as often as those who receive treatment for their mental health issues. This is unsurprising as both stress and anxiety are known to contribute significantly to the odds of a person experiencing a host of physical issues including colitis, ulcers, heart disease and more. Stress and anxiety are also known to reduce the overall strength of the immune system making those who deal with these issues in the long-term more than three times more vulnerable to a host of conditions from cancer, all the way down to the common cold.

Finally, psychological problems are also known to

dramatically increase the likelihood that sufferers will experience poor behavioral choices that can, themselves, contribute to a host of medical issues. Reckless behavior, poor eating habits, and drug or alcohol use can all be side effects of an untreated mental health condition.

Important at all ages: Every stage of life brings with it its own mental health challenges as the things that wreak havoc on a 20-year-old are very different than what that person will face when they are 55. Luckily, a lot can be done at any age to safeguard your mental health

Teens and 20s: Studies show that a majority of mental health conditions first begin to develop by the age of 25. While mental health conditions of all types are common in young people, some are far more serious and long-reaching than others. Currently, it is estimated that one in three individuals between the ages of 18 and 25 dealt with some type of mental health issue in the past year. Likewise, one in 10 individuals in that same age bracket has dealt with a mental health issue that was serious enough to impact daily activities in that same timeframe.

This period of time can be stressful for anyone as those in this age group are often moving away from home for the first time and becoming financially independent, along with all the challenges that come along with doing so. Those who are dealing with a mental health condition at this age may find these activities harder than their peers, especially as they may not yet even understand that there is anything that needs fixing because they have been dealing with the issue for their entire life.

As such, the biggest thing that those in this age range can do to effectively protect their mental health is to understand the signs of common mental health conditions and understand the importance of getting help if they see the signs in themselves. It is essential for these individuals to realize that the sooner a person starts treatment, the more effective that treatment will ultimately be. The early a person can learn healthy mental health habits the better.

30s and 40s: Those in their 30s and 40s typically have far more stress than they ever realistically expected. Building a career and building a family both require juggling a wide variety of responsibilities, and that's if you aren't trying to do both at the same time. Trying to have it all can be stressful and exhausting, two things that make it difficult to maintain mental health if it isn't given the priority it deserves.

For women, pregnancy can also cause a variety of issues when it comes to mental health, some of which can have long-term implications if left untreated. Furthermore, perimenopause, the transitional phase before menopause, tends to begin in the mid to late 40s and brings with it a variety of sudden hormonal changes that can ultimately affect physical as well as mental health.

The biggest thing those in this age bracket can do to keep their mental health going strong is not to forget to take care of themselves amidst all of the other things that are going on. This means taking important steps like bringing up potential mental health issues with your primary healthcare provider during your yearly checkup. More than merely bringing up potential issues, it is essential that you take things a step further and actually follow any advice that your doctor gives you. This is especially important if you have already been diagnosed with a specific mental health condition as these sorts of things are certainly not going to go away just because you ignore them.

Another aspect of keeping your mental health where it needs to be is ensuring that your diet is where it needs to be which can be especially challenging for those who are raising children. Nevertheless, it is the simple things that are covered in this book, getting enough sleep, exercising and eating right, that can make it easier to make it through your 30s and 40s without picking up any ongoing mental health conditions.

50s and 60s: Those in the 50s and 60s age range are likely experiencing nearly as many changes as they did when they were in the teens and 20s age bracket which can lead to an influx of stress and potential mental health issues as well. Women have experienced menopause, and both men and women who are in romantic relationships have likely seen their roles and expectations in this realm change over time. Issues like chronic illness and retirement are probably starting to approach, and those with children likely find they suddenly have an empty home for the first time in decades. All of these changes can lead to a host of mental and even physical effects.

For those in this bracket, the most important thing to do is to be proactive about your physical and mental health by rigorously sticking to the suggestions outlined in this book. It is essential to remain in regular contact with your healthcare provider during this time in your life as the more you know about the issues that are unique to you as you age, the more you can do to actively fight against the negative while doing what you can to ensure anything positive sticks around as long as possible. Likewise, it is important to remain mentally and physically active for as long as possible as activity keeps the body, as well as the mind, young.

70s and older: Those who are in their 70s and older are hopefully enjoying the full breadth of what their retirement can offer them. While this is the age that severe mental and physical health problems affect a higher percentage of the population, that doesn't mean those in this age bracket can't still enjoy all facets of life and actively work to keep away mental health issues just as they did when they were younger.

Preventative maintenance is the name of the game in this age bracket and the more a person can do to actively stave off mental issues the better.

The Fastest Way to Change How You Feel Is to Change How You Think

The sum total of all the people in the world today can be broken down into two groups, those who are always able to find success at everything they do, regardless of their mental health issues and those that, despite any skills or talents they may have, can never get over the roadblock that is their mental health issues. This is so because the first group has a mindset that encourages personal growth while the other does not.

The truth of the matter is that there are two very different ways people are raised when it comes to understanding ability and intelligence. Those who always seem to lack the motivation for success believe that talent and intelligence are innate and what you are born with is all you will ever get while the other, more successful, group believes that they are merely skills and that like any other skill they can be obtained via hard work and perseverance.

These two very different viewpoints, in turn, lead to dramatically different outlooks on life which eventually lead to remarkably different feelings towards mental health issues. While this might seem hard to believe, for some of you anyway, heading out into the world each day with the understanding that success is possible regardless of what issues you may face as long as you put in the time and effort to find it will, in fact, lead to more success over time. Known as the growth mindset, this is one thing that you can be sure all successful people have, and most of them had it instilled upon them at a very early age.

At some point during childhood, everyone is either told that they succeed because they were naturally good at things or because they worked hard and never gave up — those who are told that they were naturally gifted often developed what is known as a fixed mindset which leads to their brains being the most active when they were receiving praise for how gifted they were.

The second group can be said to have a growth mindset wherein their minds are the most active when they are learning what they could do better next time. Those with a fixed mindset tend to worry more about how others see them than what they are actually learning which is why those with a growth mindset tend to be more successful in the long run.

Fixed Mindset
- Wants to look smart or competent regardless of the reality
- Quick to avoid challenges
- Easily thwarted by obstacles
- Thinks effort is "pointless"
- Ignores feedback
- Can feel threatened by the success of others

Growth Mindset
- More interested in long-term results.
- Enjoys a challenge.
- Learns from obstacles
- Equates effort with success
- Appreciates criticism
- Finds inspiration in the success of others

To understand how the two mindsets work in action, simply remember the story of the tortoise and the hare. The hare was always told how fast he was and therefore developed a fixed mindset whereby his speed was innate and not related to his actions which meant he was free to take a nap during the race. The tortoise, on the other hand, kept a growth mindset which meant he knew that if he persevered, he would succeed. This belief in himself was born out by the results of the race.

The two mindsets also manifest themselves differently when it comes to dealing with setbacks. When those who have a fixed mindset are met with a setback, it directly affects how they see themselves because it shakes their belief in their innate talent. This makes it easier for them to give up on something they are struggling with as they can easily tell themselves that it is just not a talent that is in their wheelhouse. On the other hand, when a person with a growth mindset is met with a challenge, they instead worry about the best way to overcome it and treat the issue as an opportunity to learn and grow.

Maximize neural plasticity: If the previous paragraphs left you feeling closer to a fixed mindset individual than a person with a growth mindset, feat not. Unlike most of the rest of the human body, the brain never stops developing and changing throughout its entire lifetime. This means that thanks to this neuroplasticity, you can focus on changing your mindset for the better. While changing an innate belief will be tricky, there are a number of things you can do to ensure the process proceeds as smoothly as possible.

As with improving your discipline, changing your mindset is all about committing to the task at hand, and changing small thoughts in regards to your ability to change in general. Over time, you will be able to consciously alter larger thoughts which will then make it easier to take more active control over your mindset.

When working to keep a growth mindset in all things, it is

important to keep it up even when the going gets tough. It will likely seem like the easiest thing in the world to do while things are going well, but a fixed mindset is much more likely to manifest itself during times when roadblocks begin presenting themselves. Your fixed mindset will likely make you want to abandon all hope of forward progress when these roadblocks appear.

In this case, it is essential to make an effort to stop thinking of the challenges as roadblocks and start thinking of them as opportunities for you to learn and grow. Finding personal ways to meet the challenges that come your way head on without dwelling on them unnecessarily is the first step towards making a real change for the better.

Take a mental inventory at the end of each day: If you find that you are having difficulty keeping up a steady stream of growth mindset choices throughout the day, you may want to start keeping a log of the events that happen to you each day and what thoughts went through your head as they occurred. With the day outlined this way, you will then find it much easier to pick out the fixed mindset ideas that got through your defenses which means you will be more aware of them next time they pop up again. While it won't happen overnight, you will eventually be able to weed out a majority of your fixed mindset thoughts on a regular basis.

Empowerment is all about positivity: While you are getting used to keeping up a growth mindset on the regular, you may find that remaining positive and feeling empowered is easy as long as everything is going well, only to have things fall apart as soon as struggle is added to the equation. Those who originally had a fixed mindset are going to have a much more difficult time powering through times of adversity at first, but if they ever hope to find a way to truly empower themselves then they will need to remain positive and see it through as that is the only way that new neural pathways are ever going to be successfully formed.

Having a positive and empowered attitude doesn't mean feeling extremely positive all of the time. Everyone has days where they doubt themselves and their purpose, the difference between empowered individuals and everyone else is that those who are genuinely empowered don't let those singular instances of doubt spiral into all-consuming feelings that they then have difficulty extricating themselves from. Remember, a moment of doubt is just that, don't let a single moment define your existence, find your growth mindset and let it empower you.

CHAPTER 2: NUTRITION: HOW TO EAT SMART FOR A HEALTHIER BRAIN

When it comes to following a diet that serves to promote mental health, there is one that stands head and shoulders above the rest, especially when it comes to anxiety and depression and that is the ketogenic diet. To understand why this is the case, it is essential first, to understand a bit more about what the keto diet is all about.

Once upon a time, when humans were hunters and gatherers, they needed something besides carbohydrates to create energy when certain types of foods were not available. Over time, the liver developed the ability to produce what are known as ketones to generate energy when carbohydrates are not available. While the liver still possesses this ability, the ease with which glucose (found in high amounts in carbs) is broken down into energy, coupled with the number of carbohydrates in the average diet, means that the liver rarely has a chance to shine.

The ketogenic diet aims to change this by removing a majority of the carbohydrates the body can break down on a regular basis. This, in turn, brings on what is known as a state of ketosis whereby the liver uses up excess fat (promoting weight loss) to create the energy no longer being provided by the carbohydrates. When it comes to limiting your carbohydrates, a good guideline to shoot for is to consume less than 15 net carb grams per day. To determine your net carbs, you just add up how many carbohydrates you consumed in 24 hours and then subtract that number from the amount of fiber you consumed during that same amount of time.

To understand why the keto diet is so effective when it comes to mental health, it is helpful to compare it to a more traditional diet instead. The average diet tends to include a large number of carbs, a minimal, to average, amount of protein and only small amounts of healthy fats. As such, the body continues burning glucose to provide itself with the energy it needs to keep functioning as well as it can.

The glucose in the carbs that are consumed is then broken down into a molecule known as ATP, which is where the energy in glucose actually comes from. As a byproduct of getting at the ATP, the body also creates insulin, which is useful in some ways and harmful in others. First, it helps to move the ATP throughout the body, so your cells can get the energy they need. It is then used to store whatever energy is not required at the moment in the form of fat.

On the other hand, once ketosis is achieved, and sustained for about a week, your body will start taking advantage of all of its stored fats; The stored fat is then broken down into two different molecules, glycerol, and fatty acid. Fatty acids help your body to produce ketones which replace glucose as the primary power source for your cells. In the instances where glucose is specifically needed for one reason or another glycerol steps in and fills the gap. This is especially crucial in the brain as it generates energy through what is known as gluconeogenesis.

This, then, is the root of the reason why the keto diet can help with these issues as, while the brain typically uses carbs for fuel, too much of a good thing can lead to long-term issues. In fact, prolonged exposure to extremely high levels can cause a buildup of the brain's tolerance towards insulin. This, in turn, makes it more difficult for the brain to take in the glucose that it needs for it to continue functioning at its ideal levels. As ketosis provides a healthy alternative for the brain to receive all the fuel it needs, without any of the risks, experts believe that it will see increased use in combating these and other similar issues.

Getting started

After you have decided to embrace the keto diet, it is important to remember that the early days of the process are also going to be the most difficult. Once your body starts producing ketones on the regular, however, the natural benefits of the process will kick in and make everything worth it.

Entering ketosis: While it would be nice, the fact of the matter is that it takes more than skipping a few carb heavy meals to force your body into a ketogenic state as many people have never been anywhere near it. Instead, it is likely to take at least 7 days for your body to get with the program and allow you to start feeling the benefits of ketosis. This interim period is going to be difficult, no two ways around it. Your body will begin by burning through your available reserves of glucose until there is nothing left. During this period, you are likely to experience an extreme lack of energy in addition to hunger-pains and flu-like symptoms.

While it is going to be rough, it is important to keep in mind how necessary it is and do what you can to ensure you never give in to temptation as you will only prolong the process by adding new glucose to your system. During this period, you may find that adding a small fourth meal between lunch and dinner helps to negate the worst of the effects. If that doesn't help, consider the fact that every time your stomach growls you are actively moving towards ketosis and keep this in mind when the going gets exceptionally rough. During this period, you are going to want to limit yourself to 15 grams of carbohydrates per day, maximum, if you hope to reach your goal.

You may find it helpful to test yourself throughout this process to ensure you are moving in the right direction. What you will be testing yourself for is a substance called acetone which is produced when a ketone is broken down to generate energy. You can purchase either blood or urine tests that will indicate your current ketone level which should be somewhere between .5 when you start ketosis and 3 when your body gets used to the process. You can also determine if you are in the ketogenic state if your breath begins to smell like a slightly rotten apple and tastes slightly metallic. If, when testing yourself, you find that your ketone level rises above 3 then you are going to want to increase the number of calories you are consuming per day as your body is not getting enough of the calories it needs to function at peak effectiveness.

When it comes to getting into ketosis as quickly as possible, you will find that there aren't any real tricks to the process. Instead, you are going to want to eat the right types of foods that contain the proper nutrients. For starters, you are going to want to eat plenty of healthy fats, 70 percent of your diet should be made up of healthy fats, 25 percent should be made up of lien protein, and the remaining 5 percent can be made up of carbs. 90 percent of those fats should be from healthy sources, and 10 percent can be from anywhere.

Tips for success
Start a food journal: When you are first transitioning to the

keto diet it can easily feel as though everywhere you turn only offers up delectable food choices that contain a larger number of carbs or simply too few healthy macros to get the job done. To help yourself see that this is not the case, you may want to start a food journal so that you don't lose track of any new, keto-friendly option you might come across. What's more, it will make it easier for you to catch yourself as the few extra snacks you grab during the day will really stand out when you see that you grab them every single day.

Now, this can be a potent motivational tool, and also an incredibly useful way to keep your diet in check during the early days when you are building new habits and your body is still trying to figure out just what is going on. However, it is only going to be effective if it includes absolutely everything that you actually consume which means you need to stick with it 24 hours a day, 7 days a week. A partially completed food journal is never going to be any good for anyone which means if you hope to avoid wasting your time you need to treat it as a serious commitment and dive in for the long haul.

Not waiting out your cravings: While willpower is one thing, there are physical activities that you can do to ensure that the effects of your current carbohydrate craving are as minimal and brief as possible. In fact, there is a pair of yoga moves that you can do that will make it easier to quiet your thoughts and fight your cravings at the same time.

The first of these is a simple modified forward bend from a standing position. To perform this movement, you want to start by stand roughly 12 inches from a wall, facing away from it, with your feed planted at hip-width. From there you will want to lean your back against the wall before bending your knees and folding your chest down onto your thighs. From this position, you will then want to breathe deeply between 6 and 12 times, making a special point to focus on the moments you are exhaling. When you feel the craving start to pass, you are going to want to return to a leaning position slowly. If, after 12 breaths your craving has not subsided, you will then want to return to a leaning pose and repeat the process.

The second pose that is known to help fight carbohydrate cravings is what is known as the child's pose. This pose is known to produce what many think of as a relaxed, introspective state, the purpose of which is to allow you to really look within and determine where the root of your current craving lies. After completing this exercise, you may realize that you were even hungry, to begin with.

To start, you will want to kneel on the floor while sitting on your heels. Your knees should be planted firmly at roughly hip width or whatever is comfortable. Your hands should be placed onto your thighs with your palms facing downward. Once you are in this position, you are going to want to slowly inhale and at the same time move your chest forward so that it connects with your thighs, ideally resting your head on the ground while doing so. With your head on the ground, you will then want to move your hands, so they are resting on either side of your legs with the palms facing upwards. You may hold this position until the craving subsides.

Drink more water: Being in a state of ketosis is going to naturally dehydrate your body more quickly than would otherwise be the case. This is not the only reason why you should ensure you are drinking at least a gallon of water a day if not more as doing so will also help you feel full for a prolonged period of time, a useful thing to remember if your carbohydrate cravings ever get to be too much to handle. If you are switching to the ketogenic diet especially for the lean look it can provide then you may also be interested to note that the amount of water weight that you retain actually decreases the more well-hydrated, you stay over a prolonged period of time.

Try fat bombs: With nearly all the carbs removed from your system, it is likely that you are going to feel a hole in your diet where they used to be, primarily if you need a quick snack to tide you over or are in need of a bit of extra energy. Luckily, the keto diet has you covered with what are known as fat bombs. Fat bombs are a quick and easy snack that can be either savory or sweet and is comprised of between 80 and 90 percent healthy fat. They typically include things like coconut oil, butter, seeds and sometimes nuts but the combinations are almost endless.

Not only will these healthy snacks provide you with a quick burst of energy, but they will also fill you up in a way that many carb-based snacks will not. As such they are the perfect option when you are looking for something to give you the energy to go to the gym, or you know that you won't have time for dinner until late. They are also useful in helping you hit your healthy fat quota for the day which isn't always as easy as you may expect.

While fat bombs are easy to make and quick to eat, that doesn't mean that they shouldn't also be consumed in moderation, especially when your body is still striving to reach ketosis. Early on your body might have an adverse reaction to so much healthy fat which means you will want to introduce things slowly for the easiest transition possible.

Breakfast: Spinach Frittata with Bacon

This recipe needs 5 minutes to prepare, 35 minutes to cook and will make 4 servings.

- Fat: 79 percent
- Protein: 19 percent
- Carbs: 2 percent

What to Use
- Pepper (to taste)
- Salt (to taste)
- Butter (2 T grass fed)
- Cheese (5 oz. shredded)
- Bacon (5 oz.)
- Spinach (.5 lbs. fresh)
- Heavy whipping cream (1 cup)
- Eggs (8 large)

What to Do
- Start by making sure your oven is heated to 350 degrees F.
- Grease a baking dish using grass-fed butter.
- Add the butter to a frying pan before placing it on the stove on top of a burner set to a medium/high heat before adding in the bacon and letting it fry until it reaches your desired level of crispiness and then add in the spinach.
- In a separate mixing bowl combine the cream and the eggs before whisking well.
- Add the results to the prepared baking dish before adding in the spinach and the bacon and topping with the shredded cheese.
- Place the baking dish in the oven and let it bake 25 minutes. Let the frittata cool 5 minutes before removing from baking dish.

Lunch: Avocado and Chili Bake

This recipe needs 25 minutes to prepare, 40 minutes to cook and will make 4 servings.

- Fat: 86 percent
- Protein: 10 percent
- Carbs: 3 percent

What to Use-Crust

- Water (.25 cups)
- Egg (1 large)
- Coconut oil (3 T)
- Salt (1 pinch)
- Baking powder (1 tsp.)
- Psyllium husk (1 T powdered)
- Coconut flour (.25 cups)
- Sesame seeds (.25 cups)
- Almond flour (.75 cups)

What to Use-Filling
- Cheese (1.25 cups shredded)
- Cream cheese (.5 cups)
- Salt (.25 tsp.)
- Onion powder (.5 tsp.)
- Chili pepper (1 chopped, seeded)
- Cilantro (2 T chopped)
- Eggs (3 large)
- Mayonnaise (1 cup)
- Avocado (2 peeled, pitted)

What to Do
- Start by making sure your oven is heated to 350 degrees F.
- Combine the ingredients for the dough together using a food processor and process vigorously until they form a ball of dough.
- Line a 12-inch springform and place the dough into it before placing the dough into the oven and letting it bake 15 minutes.
- Combine the remaining ingredients in a mixing bowl and mix well before filling the crust.
- Place the springform back into the oven and let it cook for 35 minutes.

Snack: Parmesan Zucchini Tomato Gratin

This recipe needs 10 minutes to prepare, 40 minutes to cook and will make 6 servings.

- Fat: 88 percent
- Protein: 10 percent
- Carbs: 2 percent

What to Use
- Basil (2 tsp.)
- Garlic powder (1 tsp.)
- Salt (.5 tsp.)
- Garlic (2 T minced)
- Olive oil (2 T)
- Onion (.5 c chopped)
- Parmesan cheese (.5 c shredded)
- Tomatoes (2)
- Zucchini (3)

What to Do
- Ensure your oven is preheated to 350F.
- Sauté onions until translucent and fragrant. Add garlic, sautéing 1 to 2 minutes longer. Pour mixture into the bottom of a casserole dish.
- With a knife, slice tomatoes and zucchinis.
- Layer zucchini and tomatoes, alternating layers.
- Drizzle veggies with olive oil, sprinkle with seasonings and cover with Parmesan cheese.
- Bake 40 minutes until gratin turns a light brown.

Dinner: Grilled Pork Chops

This recipe needs 15 minutes to prepare, 40 minutes to cook and will make 6 servings.

- Fat: 77 percent
- Protein: 19 percent
- Carbs: 3 percent

What to Use
- Scallions (6)
- Salt (.5 tsp.)
- Pepper (to taste)
- Avocados (2 mashed)
- Green beans (.75 lbs.)
- Olive oil (2 T)
- Pork shoulder chops (4)
- Olive Oil (2 T)
- Chipotle paste (2 T)
- Onion (.5 chopped)

What to Do
- Start by making sure your oven is heated to 400 degrees F.
- In a small mixing bowl combine the chipotle, salt and oil and mix well.
- Add the results to the pork and let it sit for 15 minutes to marinate.
- Place the pork on a baking sheet and let it bake for 30 minutes, turning after 15 minutes.
- While the pork cooks add the oil to a frying pan before placing it on the stove over a burner set to a medium heat before adding in the beans and letting them cook 5 minutes. For the last minute turn the heat to low and season as desired.
- Add the onion and the avocado into the beans to warm and season as needed before plating with the pork chops.

Dessert: Walnut Orange Chocolate Bombs

This recipe needs 20 minutes to prepare, 3 hours to freeze and will make 8 servings.

- Fat: 85 percent
- Protein: 11 percent

- Carbs: 4 percent

What to Use
- Extra virgin coconut oil (.25 c)
- Orange peel or orange extract (.5 T)
- Walnuts (1.75 c chopped)
- Cinnamon (1 tsp.)
- Stevia (10-15 drops)
- Cocoa dark chocolate (12 5g 85%)

What to Do
- Melt chocolate with your choice of method.
- Add cinnamon and coconut oil. Sweeten mixture with stevia.
- Pour in fresh orange peel and chopped walnuts.
- In a muffin tin or in candy c, spoon in mixture.
- Place into the fridge for 1-3 hours until mixture is solid.

CHAPTER 3: WHAT ARE THE MENTAL HEALTH BENEFITS OF EXERCISE?

While everyone knows that exercise is good for the body, many people will be surprised to learn that it is one of the most effective means of improving your mental health as well. In fact, exercising just four days a week has been proven to have a seriously positive effect on ADHD, anxiety, depression and more. It has even been shown to boost mood, sleep better and improve memory. What's more, research shows that you don't even need to be a fitness fanatic; it only takes a regular amount of moderate exercise to reap the full range of benefits.

To understand how exercise benefits mental health, it is essential to understand that it is really about more than merely muscle size and aerobic capacity. While it can certainly add years to your life and help you look and feel great, these are not the reasons that motivate a majority of people to exercise regularly. In fact, most people who exercise on a regular basis do so because it gives them a terrific sense of well-being that cannot easily be replicated through other means. When they get their regular fix of exercise, they tend to be more energetic overall, sleep better, remember things more easily and generally have a better overall mindset which just so happens to line up with a majority of the things a person can do to help themselves overcome a variety of mental health challenges.

Fights depression: When it comes to fighting depression, studies show that exercise can actually fight both mild and moderate depression just as effectively as traditional antidepressant medication. What's more, it has also been shown to be an effective means of preventing those who find it difficult to remain out of negative thought cycles for good from relapsing once and for all.

Exercise is an excellent way to effectively combat depression for a variety of reasons, starting with the fact that it actively promotes growth in the brain that is difficult for depression to overcome. This growth also has been shown to reduce inflammation while at the same time creating new activity patterns that naturally prioritize activities and experiences that promote feelings of well-being and happiness.

At the same time, it releases endorphins which naturally stabilize your mood in the long-term in addition to making you feel noticeably better in the short-term. Finally, outside of all of that, exercise can serve as an effective distraction, giving the brain a much-needed break from the troubles of the day, breaking it free of the cycle of depression in the process.

Exercise and anxiety: Exercise is also a natural counter to anxiety as well. It is an effective means of relieving stress, as well as tension, while at the same time boosting mental and physical well-being. It is also shown to enhance well-being via the release of endorphins. Generally speaking, anything that gets you up and moving can help, but it will be more effective if whatever you are doing requires your full attention. For example, you will get more out of the experience if you take the time to pay attention to the sound as your feet hit the ground or the way the wind feels as it cools your sweaty skin. By taking the extra time to really focus on how your body feels you will find that not only are you more effective at whatever it is you are doing, but you will also be able to interrupt the steady stream of thoughts flowing through your head as well.

Stress and exercise: When the body is under stress the first thing that occurs is that the muscles in the shoulders, neck and face tense up, leading to neck and back pain, and possibly even chronic headaches if left untreated. Furthermore, if left untreated for a prolonged period of time it can lead to more severe issues like muscle cramps, tightness in the chest and high blood pressure. In severe cases, it can even lead to things like chronic diarrhea, stomachache or heartburn — the discomfort and worry that these physical symptoms cause can, in turn, lead to even greater stress, compounding the issues between mind and body in a vicious cycle that can be difficult to break free of once it begins.

Exercise is a great way to short-circuit this cycle before it gets going. Besides just releasing endorphins to the brain, regular exercise helps to relax the muscles, relieving this sort of tension before it can cause more noticeable issues. As the body and mind are closely linked, when the body feels better you will find that the mind does as well.

ADHD and exercise: Exercise is a great way to mitigate negative ADHD symptoms; so much so, some people can even use it as a complete replacement for traditional steroid treatment options. Exercise is a great choice for those looking for an extra way to curb bad habits as it helps the brain build up its ability to sustain attention, inhibit nonproductive thoughts, decrease impulsiveness, prioritizing actions and improving both memory and event sequencing.

While the innate repetition and mental discipline required

to exercise regularly can help build positive habits, most of the benefits exercise has on ADHD comes from the chemicals the brain releases while exercising. The most important of these are endorphins which are vital to helping the brain moderate pain, pleasure and overall mood. Exercise also causes the release of serotonin, norepinephrine and dopamine, three chemicals which improve attention and focus.

This doesn't mean that those with ADHD need to spend all day every day in a gym, however; instead, walking for as little as thirty minutes in a row can activate all of the chemicals discussed above. Doing so five days a week will allow you to keep a higher level of them in your system at all times. Exercise that involves group participation and teamwork is especially beneficial.

PTSD and exercise: Recent studies show that focusing on the feelings associated with exercise at the moment can help those who are dealing with PTSD to move beyond the immobilizing stress that can characterize PTSD or related trauma for some people. Rather than letting the mind wander while exercising, those who are dealing with these issues are encouraged to pay closer attention to the physical sensations of every part of the body that is involved in the exercise both inside and out. As such, exercises that involve some type of cross-movement are considered the most effective.

Getting started

If you haven't exercised regularly in quite some time, it can be difficult to get back on the horse, even if you aren't dealing with any mental health issues at the moment and things don't get any easier if you are depressed, anxious, or stressed. This can leave you in a catch-22 scenario where you know that exercising will make you feel better eventually, but you don't have the motivation or energy to get up off the couch and make your way to the gym. Luckily, the most difficult thing to do is actually making the decision to take charge of your life and start exercising once more, so once that is taken care of you are already off to the races.

Start small: If you are dealing with some type of mental health issue, and you also haven't exercised regularly in six months or more, then starting small isn't just a valid option, it is the smart choice. Biting off too much too soon when exercising can be dangerous, in addition to being a great way to burn yourself out and ensure you end up not exercising for another six months sooner rather than later. What's worse, if you don't live up to your unrealistic expectations then you risk exacerbating your mental health issue even more and creating a self-perpetuating cycle of failure. Instead, it is far better to set mild goals that you know that you can hit to build your self-confidence as you go until you can set a goal that tests your mettle without having to worry about losing your confidence if you fall short.

Know yourself: If you are turning to exercise as a means of helping you deal with an existing mental health issue, then it is important that you take the time to understand when your natural energy levels are highest so you can use that energy to exercise. It doesn't matter if this point comes in the middle of the morning or in the middle of the night, if you are hoping to build the right exercise habits then it is essential to use this time productively until you get into enough of a habit that you will still be able to ensure you stick with it if you move things to a more reasonable time.

If anxiety or depression has you feeling unmotivated and tired day in and day out, something as simple as going for a walk or dancing to your favorite song could be enough to energize you. While it might not seem like it, give it a try, you will be surprised at the results. As you move and start to feel a little better, you'll experience a greater sense of control over your well-being. You may even feel energized enough to kick things up a notch and exercise more vigorously—by walking further, breaking into a run, or adding a bike ride to the mix.

Avoid caffeine: While coffee and energy drinks are not inherently negative, if you drink something with caffeine in it to start every single morning, your body loses its ability to create the proper chemicals to wake you up. Drinking coffee means the drink is doing the work for your body, so it doesn't need to do it any longer. That means it won't even try to wake you up if the coffee will do it instead. What's worse, anxiety and depression are often strongly linked which means that drinking too much caffeine might do more than make you anxious; it could make you more depressed as well.

Instead, you should replace that negative caffeine habit with a regular, early morning exercise routine. Working out is not the way most people want to start their day. It's a lot of effort early in the morning, and that's understandably not appealing. But the fact is, you don't need to run a marathon in the morning to get the benefits of its wake-up powers. Instead, you can start your day with a dozen or so push-ups or sit-ups, or a jog around the block. Each of these should take you less than ten minutes and will force your tired and achy body to kick into gear right away. Just by exerting some effort in the wee hours of the morning will get your body going and make the rest of your morning easier than you could ever imagine.

Don't forget to stretch: Stretching is one of the most flexible types of exercise one can do (no pun intended). If you have twenty seconds in your schedule, stretch your arms or back to get a nice little relaxing boost of energy. If you have several hours of time to spare, take up a yoga class and learn to participate in some real intense stretching for long stretches of time (again, no pun intended).

10-minute-high intensity workout

This exercise plan is easy to get started with as you don't need anything special but the determination to stick with it every day. You will want to pick several exercises from the list below and then complete the entire circuit three times, with a 10-second rest between each set. Each circuit should take 3 minutes and 10 seconds.

Sumo squats: Start with your feet at slightly more than hip-width apart and keep your toes pointed facing outward at a 45-degree angle. Place all of your weight on the heels of your feet, your chest upright and your back straight, lower yourself down towards the ground until your thighs are substantially parallel to the ground. Using your quads and your glutes, push yourself back into the starting position. To end each set, move into a reverse lung and fold your body forward while keeping your arms stretched overhead.

Side plank: To begin this exercise assume a standard push-up position before lifting one hand off of the ground and turning to that side. Hold this position for as long as you can remain safe and hold your form correctly. This exercise can be strenuous if you have not previously strengthened the required muscle groups, you can begin practicing this move leaning to one side and raising one arm slightly off the ground. It will be difficult to find your balance at first, keep at it. This exercise benefits the core and leg muscles.

Jumping jacks: Start by standing in a relaxed stance, with your feet about hip-width apart and your arms resting at your sides. Jump up while spreading your feet and raising your arms above your head. Repeat as many times as possible, as quickly as possible, for about 45 seconds. If keeping this up for the full length of time proves untenable, get your body used to the exercise by following through with the movement and leaving out the jumping.

Jab, cross, front kick (left): Start with your left foot in front of your right foot and your hips facing right. Raise your arms so that you are in somewhat of a boxer stance. Start with a jab by punching forward with your left arm straight out. Move directly into throwing across by punching with your left arm and rotating your body to the right. This should leave the full weight of your body on your right foot, and your right heel should raise slightly off of the floor. End the sequence by kicking forward with your back foot.

Jab, cross front kick (right): The same as above but in reverse.

Leg drop: Begin by lying flat on your back with your legs pointing straight up. From there, lower one leg at a time in a fluid movement before returning it to the starting position. Remember to keep your legs straight at all times, and when lowering each leg, you should stop just before it touches the ground. This exercise benefits the core.

Hip bridge: Begin this exercise lying on your back with knees bent but with both of your feet on the floor. Lift your hips while at the same time squeezing your buttocks while attempting to create a straight line from your shoulders to your knees. To make this exercise more difficult, keep one foot on the floor while lifting the other, so it is pointing at the ceiling. Switch legs halfway through. This exercise improves hip flexibility while strengthening the back and stretching the spine.

Triceps back dips: To do this exercise properly you will need a low bench to support yourself against. To begin this exercise stand facing away from the bench you will be using. Place your hands behind you, so they are resting on the bench before moving your feet forward slightly and bending your knees so you lower yourself as close to the ground as possible while still remaining your balance. Ensure that you maintain proper form by keeping the elbows tight to your sides. This exercise benefits the shoulders and back.

CHAPTER 4: HOW GRATITUDE CAN IMPROVE YOUR MENTAL HEALTH

While there is no one out there who would argue that being grateful is a bad thing, most will still be surprised at just how useful it can be when it comes to improving both physical and mental health. The first reason for this is as simple as the fact that experiencing gratitude can warm the heart and increase happiness which has been proven to aid in the healing of a wide variety of illnesses.

There are likewise a wide variety of ways to experience this little boost in happiness from keeping a gratitude journal to simply saying aloud how you feel a few times per day. Regardless of how you choose to express it, gratitude's effects run far deeper thanks to the variety of neurological effects it provides.

Gratitude has positive effects on the brain: The hypothalamus is the part of the brain that helps to regulate a wide variety of bodily functions including things like growth, metabolism, temperature, sleep, and appetite. The hypothalamus naturally activates when a person feels gratitude or receives or displays kindness which means it is a core part of every person whether they choose to admit it or not.

In fact, when experiencing gratitude, the brain also releases dopamine, which should be a cue that it is important enough to warrant positive reinforcement. The idea is that, as feeling gratitude leads to positive effects (dopamine) a person would learn to take the time to be grateful on a regular basis. Over time, the cumulative neurological effects of gratitude lead to a variety of additional health benefits including the following list.

Increased pain threshold: While you may not believe that something as simple as being grateful for the things in your life that bring you joy can lead to a reduction of physical pain, a 2003 study proved just that. During the study, some hospital patients who were suffering from the same illness were split into two groups, and half of the group were asked to keep a gratitude journal regularly. The test group showed a 20 percent reduction in pain compared to the control group. It also found the grateful patients were more willing to put extra effort into their recovery and were far more willing to exercise.

Improves sleep: A wide variety of studies have shown that those who are more grateful routinely sleep for longer periods of time, fall asleep more easily and all around have a more restful night's sleep than those who are less grateful. As noted above, one of the most important things that the hypothalamus does is regulate sleep. As gratitude activates the hypothalamus, it stands to reason that professing gratitude before bed leads to a deeper, more relaxed sleep.

As sleep is such an essential part of a person's overall well-being, the positive effects of gratitude can thus be said to reach even further, as a good night's sleep is connected to a wide variety of bodily functions. Likewise, getting enough sleep can be seen as a remedy for stress, pain, depression, and anxiety. It also improves the immune system meaning that gratitude naturally helps a person live a healthier life overall.

Reduces stress: While sleeping better naturally reduces stress, being grateful goes beyond this benefit to improve the health of the nervous system and heart as well. A 2007 study found that gratitude has a notable effect on those with hypertension, and that having a person audibly count their blessings once a week is enough to noticeably decrease their systolic blood pressure. Likewise, it has been proven that keeping a gratitude journal and writing in it frequently can reduce blood pressure by as much as 10 percent. This is likely because gratitude has been proven to decrease the amount of cortisol in the system. Cortisol is the most prominent of hormones that cause stress.

Reduces depression and anxiety: Studies regarding depression and gratitude show that those who keep a daily gratitude journal regularly report being approximately 30 percent less depressed for the duration of the exercise. Likewise, a more recent study regarding anxiety and gratitude found that writing thank you letters regularly was enough to generate significant behavioral changes. MRI scans of those who took up this practice found that this was due to an increase in neural modulation due to changes in the medial prefrontal cortex. This, in turn, meant that they were able to manage negative emotions more easily while also naturally being more kind and empathetic as well.

Increased vitality: In addition to the benefits outlined above, gratitude has also been proven to lead to increased vigor and vitality. While there are a wide variety of suggestions as to why this is the case, including stronger immune systems, healthier hearts, and an increasingly positive outlook, the exact reason that this is the case is not yet clear. What is clear, however, is that people who are grateful tend to have naturally higher energy levels, have higher levels of happiness and fewer instances of illness. All told, it appears as though gratitude can potentially lengthen the average lifespan as well.

Of course, it doesn't matter if gratitude makes us healthier due to the power of positivity, or if the dopamine in our brains sets off a chain reaction that ignites the benefits of gratitude. Every study done on the subject of gratitude research has undisputable evidence that gratitude benefits body, mind, and soul.

Developing an attitude of gratitude

The next time you find yourself complaining about waiting in a long queue or being a victim of wandering thoughts such as how unfair your new boss is or how boring your job is, use it as stimulation for creating a quick mental list of the amazing things you are blessed with. These can be the smallest or tiniest things which we tend to take for granted such as our eyesight, imagination, home, food, loved ones and much more. Just look around you and realize there's so much to be thankful for. Get to work right now and make a list of 100 things that you are really blessed to have in your life. Carefully think and list down each little thing in your life that you are thankful for.

Your gratitude nuggets can include unexpected texts from an old buddy or a really friendly new client. It can be access to inspirational videos or books to funny things your kid says. Gratitude can be expressed for your best friend's sense of humor that never fails to amaze you when you are feeling low or a skill that you recently acquired. Thankfulness can be expressed for your favorite local park, where you head to for some solitude or a buzzing bar, where you chill out with your gang.

Gratitude helps us release positive vibes that create an enhanced filter of the world around us. This positive filter lets us view how wonderful things are and allows our mind to explore the world of possibilities. If you genuinely seek happiness and a life of your dreams, stop wasting precious energy on things you fear or do not want, and focus on being thankful for what you are blessed with. When you are genuinely grateful for something, you are only creating more opportunities to attract more of it in your life.

Begin your list with "I am truly thankful for" and list down every blessing under the sun (including the sun) that you can think of. Gratitude will turbo power your desires to help the universe manifest them even more quickly.

CHAPTER 5: WHY IS SLEEP SO CRUCIAL FOR YOUR BRAIN HEALTH?

Approximately thirty percent of all Americans don't get enough sleep. While caffeine is the solution to this problem by approximately 90 percent of those over the age of 16, this drug only solves the symptoms of this issue without doing anything to improve the root cause. Sleep deprivation can have a serious impact on mental health to the point that adults are recommended to try for seven hours of sleep per day to ward off potential long-term mental health effects.

Suffering through the occasional sleepless night is one thing when sleeplessness becomes an issue is when it ceases to be an isolated incident. Currently, somewhere around 40 million people are dealing with some type of chronic sleep disorder and because sleep and mental health are very closely related, it is hard to deny there is some type of connection taking place.

This connection becomes even more evident with the understanding that upwards of 80 percent of those with some sort of existing mental condition also complain of issues relating to sleep. This is especially prevalent with those who are dealing with issues relating to ADHD, anxiety, and depression. While experts long believed that these sleep disturbances were the result of the mental health issue, more recent studies show that this may not be the case.

Instead, modern research suggests that sleep issues could well be working to trigger the mental health condition or at least exacerbating what is already there. This is potentially because the average night's sleep is made up of a combination of REM and non-REM sleep. REM sleep is vital to helping the brain improve when it comes to memory, learning and even emotional health. REM sleep is only reached when an unbroken period of approximately 90 minutes occurs which means that those who regularly find themselves having difficulty sleeping may not be receiving much REM sleep on a given night despite their best efforts.

When REM sleep is disrupted for a prolonged period of time, it begins to disrupt the brains neurotransmitters which, in turn, leads to increased levels of cortisol and increased feelings of stress as a result. It is this disruption that is likely to provoke underlying mental health issues and bring them to the surface. What follows are the three main reasons why it is so important to regularly prioritize quality sleep to ensure true peace of mind.

Your brain needs a good reset: Your brain spends its time taking in a host of environmental data and performing the types of complex processing tasks that could hold up even the most expensive computers. All this work leads to a significant amount of leftover neural waste material that the brain can only get rid of with a good reset once a day. Essentially, what this means is that without the time it needs to rest, recharge, and clean itself, the brain won't be at its best when morning comes around.

The brain needs time to process experiences: Have you ever experienced an important event in your life, went to sleep, and wake up the next day surprised to find that you feel entirely different about it? This is because the brain needs time to process events that are especially meaningful so that it can determine the best course of action moving forward. Thus you can feel one way about an event in the evening and then completely different about it the next morning once your brain has had time to figure out the best course forward.

This can also be seen in people who have experienced serious trauma as they often go on to experience PTSD, but those who go to sleep soon after they experience their trauma have a far lower chance of developing the condition than those who don't sleep for 12 hours or more after the incident occurs.

Sleeping well promotes mindfulness: Making sleep a priority is also known to provide the mind with many of the same benefits that are typically associated with mindfulness. In one study, people who had trouble sleeping were taught mindfulness practices and compared to those who regularly took some type of sleeping pill. After six weeks, those who practiced mindfulness were sleeping more frequently on their own than those who took the medication.

This research shows that mindfulness can be an effective sleep aid, but it also explains why it can work the other way as well, and sleep can generate many of the same benefits as mindfulness meditation. Mindfulness meditation is all about focusing on the moment and experiencing as much of the data your senses are experiencing as fully as possible. REM sleep allows the brain to enter a similar state where it can focus solely on past experiences while taking in as little new data as possible.

Fights depression: Roughly 80 percent of those who deal with depression on a regular basis also fight against some type of sleep issue, with sleep apnea and insomnia being at the top of the list. In fact, those who deal with insomnia are nearly four times as likely to develop depression than those who do not. This is especially common in teens as sleep problems are typically a precursor to depression.

Helps with anxiety: Roughly 50 percent of those who suffer from generalized anxiety disorder also deal with regular sleep issues. Sleep and anxiety have a cyclical relationship with one another, being anxious can make it difficult to stay or fall asleep which can then lead to additional anxiety based around why the loss of sleep is happening in the first place. Low-quality rest is also known to magnify these symptoms, making them difficult to deal with if they are left untreated in the long-term.

Tips for getting a better night's sleep

There are no two ways about, sleeping better makes you more productive throughout all facets of your life. Unfortunately, while almost everyone is interested in getting a better night's sleep, actively taking steps to reliably do so can be surprisingly difficult. Consider the following tips, and you will be getting a better night's sleep before you know it.

Unplug: While it might seem surprising, one of the easiest ways to improve both the quantity and quality of sleep that you receive is to remove all of the electronics from your bedroom. This is the case for many reasons, the first of which is the fact that the blue light emitted from computers, tablets, smartphones, and televisions actually suppress the amount of melatonin that the body produces. Melatonin plays a large role in the regulation of circadian rhythms which make it easier to both fall asleep and stay asleep once you are. As such, removing these devices, and replacing the alarm on your phone with a good old-fashioned alarm clock is a great first step.

Exercise regularly: Studies shows that excrcising regularly is helpful when it comes to making your body feel ready for sleep. This doesn't need to be a full-fledged workout, something as simple as a 20-minute walk around the block can be enough to get your blood moving and improve the quality of your sleep as a result. With that being said, it is important to finish at least 2 hours prior to hitting the hay to give your body plenty of time to wind down and prepare for sleep after the fact.

Get into a routine: Studies show that a full 75 percent of all adults don't go to bed at the same time every night. If you are looking to get a better night's sleep then setting up a schedule and getting your body into the habit of sleeping for a set period of time is a great way to do so. After just two weeks of adopting a regular sleep schedule, most people not only report that it is easier for them to fall asleep, they also report sleeping better overall as well.

Dealing with persistent nightmares: Habitual nightmares can trigger anxiety related to sleep that can lead to additional disorders, in addition to making anxiety of all types more severe as the body is already running in a compromised state. This prolonged sleep debt can lead to a deficit in cognitive function, memory lapses and emotional instability, which will, in turn, lead to an increase in the presentation of anxiety symptoms.

When done correctly, nightmare exposure and rescripting combines the traditional ideas behind exposure therapy with additional emotional processing of the core event to reduce the overall anxiety that is felt about the situation in question, and thus the ancillary incidents as well. Rescripting is also known to be beneficial when it comes to dealing with more everyday negative experiences that lead to sadness or frustration. Studies show that this technique can significantly reduce the frequency of related nightmares if it is used correctly and on a strict schedule until results are achieved.

The first step is going to be the most difficult, as it is going to involve looking back at the inciting incident and deciding what about it is the cause of the issues that have developed as a result. The specific issues that you uncover are going to be different for everyone, and you may need professional help to deal with them appropriately. When you are ready to unpack the issue successfully, however, you are going to have to confront the dream repeatedly.

What was the worst part of your dream? While this might be a difficult thing to confront directly, the only way you can ever expect to change your dreams is if you understand them fully. Even if you have been dealing with the same dream for years, you will be surprised how writing it down will help to give it shape and make all of the details stand out in your mind. Once you have fully described the details of your nightmare, the next thing you will want to do is to apply the same descriptive methods to any real-life experiences that may be influencing your dream. Don't be stingy with the details here, the more possibilities you can come up with, the better.

Next, you are going to want to compare the two, taking special notes of their differences. When you are in a dream, there are often inconsistencies in the plot or the world that will give them away, but only if you are alert enough to look for them. Not only will looking at the differences between dreams and reality make it easier for you to disregard the issues that your dreams bring up, but it will also make it easier for you to notice them in your dreams and wake yourself up as a result.

Once you have a list of negative events that you experience in your nightmare, the next thing you are going to want to do is to consider the feelings and experiences that you have during the nightmare. Try and make a list that is as complete as possible. With your list completed, you are then going to want to go through each, one by one, and come up with a positive experience that you would prefer to have in its place. These alternative experiences should be as detailed as possible, including sensory data and descriptive imagery.

Once you have a list of negative events that you experience in your nightmare, the next thing you are going to want to do is to consider the feelings and experiences that you have during the nightmare. Try and make a list that is as complete as possible. With your list completed, you are then going to want to go through each, one by one, and come up with a positive experience that you would prefer to have in its place.

You will then want to start by writing down an account of the dream, not as it typically occurs, but as you would like it to occur instead. Rather than taking a turn for the worst, write out a narrative that sees the dream play out in a positive, if uneventful way. You are going to want to write this narrative right before you fall asleep, and be sure to physically write it out to give the thought some extra substance.

Finally, all that is left to do is go to sleep. While it is unlikely that the first time that you write down your dream, it is going to do you any good, you will find that with practice you will, slowly but surely, start to see more of your dream play out the way it does in your narrative. You are going to want to continue to write down the script for the dream every night, and make sure not to get discouraged if you have success at one point and then backslide.

CHAPTER 6: HOW TO FIGHT ANXIETY AND DEPRESSION WITHOUT MEDICATION

Cognitive behavioral therapy, more commonly known as CBT has a long history of being effective for some people when it comes to dealing with their depression or anxiety. The core assumption of CBT is that the way that a person feels is directly related to that person's pattern of thoughts. If those thoughts are negative, then they are going to affect that person's mood negatively, impacting their sense of self, their behavior, and even their overall physical state. The goal with CBT, then, is to help those with depression learn to recognize their negative thoughts as well as healthy ways of dealing with them.

Additionally, therapists who work with CBT typically strive to help their patients change patterns of behavior that tend to come along with many types of dysfunctional thinking. These patterns often lead to inescapable downward spirals for those with depression which is why changing behavior is so vital to successfully changing mood.

In general, CBT is recommended for those with either moderate or mild feelings of depression or anxiety, and many report a significant decrease in their overall symptoms without having to resort to any medication whatsoever. For those with more severe issues, CBT can still be a viable part of a larger overall treatment plan that will likely still involve some form of medication in most cases. CBT is also useful for children and teens who are experiencing depression or anxiety along with others who cannot, or chose not to take traditional medications.

In fact, nearly 60 percent of patients who were treated via CBT were able to experience a noticeable decrease in their feelings of depression without having to resort to any additional treatment options. It is also useful for those who have mostly gotten their depression under control but are having trouble dealing with a few lingering issues. While a wide variety of people are sure to respond to CBT to some extent or another, those who are likely going to get the most out of it are going to be naturally motivated to seek improvement, understand that they are in control of their own actions and already have the capacity for easy introspection.

CBT is chockablock with various techniques and exercise designed to make you stop and think about your response to a given situation before you go through with it. This level of flexibility is fundamental because it means they can be practiced as part of a daily regiment designed to keep you functioning at a normal level and also during periods of extreme stress or when your triggers are unavoidable.

When you first start practicing, above all else, it is essential to keep in mind that you are developing new skills to help you deal with your specific issues which mean that, as with any other skill, it is going to take time to develop fully. Keeping this in mind is important, as the first few times you try many of these exercises you likely won't succeed and having unrealistic expectations up front can make it more difficult to pick yourself up and try again.

Keep a journal: CBT is all about becoming aware of your personal patterns, determining if they are beneficial and jettisoning them if this turns out to not be the case. Even if you do not know what you are looking for yet, merely keeping a list of all of the activities and tasks you complete on a daily basis can ultimately prove extremely useful.

Not only will having a record of your recent past prove useful moving forward, but it will also help you to get used to expressing the way that the issues you are struggling with make you feel. Many people have trouble opening up to a therapist at first, simply because they have never articulated the way their issues make them feel out loud before. Forcing yourself to put it all down on paper is a great first step to expressing yourself in a way that makes it possible for other people to understand what you are going through.

You are going to want to use the ABCD model for describing your experiences. First, you will list the activating event, including an explanation of the situation, with all personal bias removed, this should just state the facts. You will also want to make note of the first thing crossed your mind when the event occurred as this is likely an automatic thought which means knowing it could be useful later. From there, you will want to write down any beliefs that came into play as well, starting with the type of negative thoughts you experienced. If possible, you are also going to want to write down the source of the belief as well.

From there, you are going to want to write down the relevant consequences that occurred from the way you handled the incident, both short and long-term. Finally, if possible, you are going to want to dispute your negative thoughts and replace them with alternatives that you could have used instead. It is essential to get into the habit of writing in your journal at the end of every single day as almost every exercise described in the following chapters can benefit from having a more complete idea of what the relationship between various actions, events and emotions might be.

When dealing with CBT, it is impossible to have too much information about what is going on in your daily life, the more events you write down each day, the better. While initially, you may have a difficult time remembering the finer details of the things that happen to you throughout the day, it is essential to keep up the practice regardless. Over time you will find that you are more easily able to remember these types of details, but until then you may want to take notes after a noteworthy experience occurs, just to be sure you get everything right.

With enough of your thoughts written down, you will be able to nip these negative thoughts in the bud before they cause you to take actions or feel emotions that you will later regret. Furthermore, you will likely be surprised at how often merely being aware of the cognitive distortion at the moment is enough to mitigate it completely. This is unlikely to work with all forms of cognitive distortion, however, especially those that are exceptionally deeply ingrained in your psyche which is where the other exercises found in this book are likely to come in handy.

Train your anxiety with improved responses: Training your anxiety to only respond to appropriate cues is all about getting into a mindset where you understand that your anxiety is something that works for you, not the other way round. To do so, the first thing you need to do is to understand that the issue isn't that you feel anxiety in the first place, after all, it is a useful feeling in many circumstances. No, the real issue is that you feel anxiety more severely and frequently than is necessary to you living your best life. In early humans, anxiety was used as a means of alerting them to danger when their survival could potentially be on the line. It is only when it gets out of hand that it goes from helping to harming, which is why it is so essential to reign it in and teach it the appropriate time to manifest itself.

The secret to anxiety is that it only really manifests itself when the body triggers the types of responses that indicate a threat, regardless of whether that threat is real or imagined. As such, if you want to train your anxiety to be more selective, then you are going to need to be mindful of providing it with the type of feedback it requires in order to understand that everything is currently hunky dory. To do so in the best way possible, the first thing you will need to do is to assess the types of responses you are experiencing the next time you start to feel an anxiety attack coming on.

After you are able to determine the types of physical triggers that are setting off your personal issues, you will then be able to know what you can do to work to counteract those triggers at the moment to cut your anxiety off at the knees. If you can manage this trick successfully, then you should be able to convince yourself that everything is fine, negating the need for it to exist in the first place. To do so you are going to want to do things like prioritizing open body language, speak in a calm, measured vice, smile, and breath slowly and deeply.

Positive Self-Talk: When you're bogged down with worry and doubt, if you start to think less of yourself. "I can't do this" or "I'm a horrible person" or "I screw everything up" play over and over in your head like a mantra. This repetition has a deep impact on you that you may not realize: the more you think or say these things, the more you come to believe it. What goes from giving yourself a hard time become redefining how you actually see yourself. You may even let these thoughts out in the form of words.

To push back against this, there's something called "positive self-talk." It's an exercise wherein you notice you're having a negative thought, or you say something negative about yourself, and you try to substitute it with a positive. It requires you to pay attention to yourself (which is good—it's self-awareness!) and react as soon as you realize you're browbeating yourself. At first, you won't be substituting the thoughts and words so much as reacting to them, but in time you can become so good at recognizing this misplaced negativity that you'll almost be two steps ahead and can actually literally substitute them.

It's understandable if you're a little uncomfortable approaching this at first. If that's the case, you can start with a different approach that can be incorporated into your journal writing if you like. Take some time to jot down the negative thoughts that occur in your mind, the "I can't" and "I won't" phrases that are holding you back. For each one, write a positive opposite next to it that you can use to curtail the thought. Think of it in realistic terms: instead of saying "I can't do this," try "I didn't do this before, but I will now." Keep the list tucked away in your pocket throughout the day and refer to it as needed to remind yourself of how you should be thinking.

Funeral Exercise: The primary aim of CBT is to keep your attention on the present moment as a means to stop yourself from wandering into the unknown mists of the future—the "ifs" and "whys" that plant seeds of fear that bloom into uncontrolled anxiety. To this end, CBT exercises train you to focus on the immediate now: what you're doing now, what's around you now, how you're feeling now and why. The proven methods are published in studies and workbooks shared among those working in the field, so common exercises are well-known among therapists and patients alike.

In this section, we're going to explore an exercise that goes against all this. In itself, it doesn't have origins in CBT so much as general self-help, and while it relates to overcoming our anxiety in the same way that fear-setting does, it isn't something that's widely accepted or even recognized by therapists. It's something that you'll want to practice on your own (for reasons we'll discuss) but before you do its best you discuss it with your therapist first. Everyone responds to this differently, and emotional responses can be extreme. Thus, you'll want your therapist to weigh in on how you've been doing recovery wise, how well you've adapted to your regular CBT exercises, and how they think you're ready to handle this.

We're going to talk about the funeral exercise as made popular by author and mentor Michael Hyatt.

Overtime anxiety forces us to focus on the unknown possibilities that may lie before us. It prompts us to try and deal with them as though they were certainties, so much so that we lose sight of what actually is certain—the immediate now. With the funeral exercise, we'll be breaking one of the rules of CBT and focusing on the future. But rather than picking a scenario that could with varying levels of likelihood, we're going to focus on what is inevitable—the end. Death is a certainty. What we don't know, however, is how we get there. For the funeral exercise, you'll be envisioning your idealized funeral and how you want to get there. It sounds grim, I know, but it will make more sense as we go over the steps.

You'll want to do this in private for a variety of reasons, so find a quiet place free of distractions: no television, no computer, no music, and no games. Anything that could take your mind off the task at hand needs to removed. You will need, at the minimum, paper and something to write with. You'll want to be comfortable because as detailed writing this takes some time, so keep that in mind.

When you're comfortable and ready to begin, start by imagining your own funeral. It's (hopefully!) a long way off, but it is inevitable. This is where privacy becomes really important. For some people, this and the following steps bring up a lot of emotions they weren't necessarily expecting. It helps if you express these things as they come, but it could be awkward to do so if there are people around, even those you are close to. Feel free to let it all out at any point in the process. With that said, you should also know your limits. If it becomes too difficult or painful, or if you sense you are moving towards a bad frame of mind while going through these steps, please stop. It is possible that if you aren't prepared thinking about these things could take worse your anxiety or other mental health concerns.

With your funeral imagined, think about who you hope would attend. Keep this moment in the "now" by focusing on the people who are or who have been in your life and not those you have no real acquaintance with. It can take some time to determine which relationships you feel are the most important and those that you don't, so start making use of your paper here if need be. Most of us can rattle off a list of names without trouble—friends and family are always a good place to start—but take the time to really think about it as to not leave anyone out of the event.

With everyone named and imagined, give each one some time to speak. Here's where we get speculative: what would you want them to say if given a chance? How would you want to be remembered? What is the impact that you want to leave on each of these people?

People like to think that we have no control over how we're remembered, and there is an amount of truth to this in that we cannot control the thoughts of others. But our actions influence how we are seen just as they influence how we feel. So, if you want to be remembered fondly (as we all do, I would hope), it's entirely possible. Envision what that is like and write down what each person would say at your funeral.

Now we get to the meat of the matter. You've seen the end how you'd like it to be. Now it's time to figure out how you get those people to say those things, how you leave that sort of mark on each person in your life. Jot down what you can do now to leave the impression you want on those you hold dear. What is it that you need to do before then, and with the rest of your life, to be remembered how you want? What changes need to be made, and how can you make them?

This can be a real eye-opening experience; we often don't see how the path from A to B can be built in reverse, but that's exactly what the funeral exercise is about. Though we are looking ahead briefly, it's really just as a means to reflect on the ever-important present. As with the CBT exercises, this can be done again and again (Hyatt claims to rewrite his list through the year), and the more you practice, the easier it becomes. It's also possible to incorporate other CBT practices into the funeral exercise to make.

CHAPTER 7: HOW TO REDUCE STRESS WITH MINDFULNESS MEDITATION

Meditation is a skill everyone's heard of, but many people really don't understand. In the West, we often think of meditation as a spiritual or mystical practice, and while it's true that meditation has been used in various religious practices in its most basic form, it is a simple thought exercise. Mindfulness meditation teaches us to focus and occupy the space between our thoughts rather than on those thoughts. As we come to recognize these peaceful moments we can use meditation to go back to them. It's a great tool made even more powerful by the fact that it can be done anywhere in any situation. All it takes is practice.

While it has been a part of the Buddhist faith for more than two thousand years, mindfulness meditation has started to catch on in the west over the past few decades thanks to a proven ability to improve mental health, including anxiety, stress and even drug addiction. Professor Jon Kabat-Zinn brought the process to the attention of the modern world in the 1970s by publishing his findings show how it was related to a dramatic reduction in both stress and anxiety.

This, in turn, leads to a renewed interest in the practice

and a new understanding of the many ways that being mindful can improve one's health by directly getting to the heart of many of the issues that are caused by anxiety in the first place. Studies on the topic have actually proven so successfully that mindfulness meditation is now being used in a wide variety of governmental institutions in the US including prisons and VA hospitals.

While looking inside yourself in hopes of finding an untapped well of tranquility and inner peace might seem like a stretch, the fact of the matter is that you can undoubtedly become proficient at the practice regardless if you believe in its efficacy. All you need to do is keep it up every day, and ensure you try your hardest to do what is required of you. Luckily, this really shouldn't be too hard as after you get the basics down you will find that you can practice being mindful virtually anywhere you can commit yourself to be as fully present at the moment as possible.

Studies have shown time and time again that those who practice meditation are better able to manage stress, and studies focusing on anxiety disorders have shown direct positive improvement. Simply put, meditation has a real, measurable effect. However, to reap these benefits, you need to meditate regularly, not just when you're feeling anxious. Think of it as a muscle, the more often you use it, the stronger it becomes.

Mindfulness meditation is also useful as, once you get the hang of it, it can be used practically at any time regardless of whatever else you are doing. Initially, however, you are going to want to block out 10 or 15 minutes where you can practice finding the proper mindset.

Getting started

Starter practice: For just a few minutes, take a seat. It need not be in a chair, nor do you need to sit with your legs positioned in a specific way. Simply sit down with your back straight. Put your hands in your lap and close your eyes. Then, breathe slowly. When you do, focus all of your attention on how breathing itself feels. Really fixate on the senses: the air entering and exiting your nostrils or mouth; the expansion of your lungs, how cold or warm the air is. When these few minutes are up, open your eyes and examine how you feel physically and mentally. Try this once a day, extending the time a little bit each day.

Full practice: Once you have improved your breathing, the next thing is to pair the exercise with a conscious effort to remove all thoughts from your mind. Once you have reached a relaxed state, to remove the excess thoughts that are likely running through your head, all you need to do is picture them as a stream of bubbles that are rushing by in front of your eyes. Simply take a step back and let the thoughts flow past you without interacting with them. If one of them catches your attention and draws you into more complex thought, simply disengage and let it go. Don't focus on the fact that you were thinking about it, because that will just draw you out of the moment, simply remain in that state for as long as possible. Eventually, this will help with negative thoughts you experience in the real world as well.

In fact, with enough time and practice, you will likely find that you are able to maintain a mild meditative state even when you are otherwise focused on the world around you. This is known as a state of mindfulness, and it should be the end goal of everyone who is new to the meditative practice. Being mindful means always being connected to a calming and soothing mental state as well as one that is full of joy and peace which benefits not just yourself but everyone around you.

Research shows that practicing mindfulness regularly can

improve brain health as well as function and starting young will ensure your brain retains more volume as you age. Those who regularly practice mindfulness will also find they have a thicker hippocampus and as a result have an easier time learning and retaining more information. They will also notice that the part of the amygdala which controls fear, anxiety, and stress is less active. With all of these physical changes to the brain is it any wonder that those who practice mindfulness report a general increase in well-being and mood?

Don't judge the way you feel: When you first begin your mindfulness meditation practice, you will likely find that your mind is always trying to insert thoughts into the space within your mind that you are trying to create. This is because your brain has learned to always jump from one thought to another over the years and it is a habit that is certainly not doing your anxiety any favors.

Other ways to practice mindfulness

On your commute: By practicing mindfulness meditation on the road, you will find that you arrive at work ready to meet the challenges of the day head-on without being angry about them and arrive home at the end of the day with a clear head and heart, with the cares of the day left somewhere on the turnpike. Practicing mindfulness meditation on the go will allow you to reach your destination in a calm and focused state, that allows the stresses of rush hour traffic to fade into the background. What's more, practicing mindfulness meditation will also ensure you drive as safely as possible because you will be entirely focused on the moment and the traffic that surrounds you.

To make the most of your commute, you are going to want to practice mindfulness from the very first moment that you enter your vehicle. As such, the first thing that you will want to do is to announce your intention aloud to the universe to help you get into the right mindset from the start.

With your intentions made plain, the next thing that you are going to want to do (even before starting your vehicle) is to take several deep breaths. This will allow you to focus your attention on the sensations that your senses are providing you in order to ensure that you are in the right mindset even before you hit the road.

During this period, you want to take special care to focus on your body and the way it feels as you sit in your seat, the way your hands feel on the steering wheel and the way the world around you looks as you stare out at it from behind the windshield. From there, let the sensations of feeling expand outward and downward so that you feel your feet and the pressure you exert on the pedals before starting your vehicle.

Being mindful while doing chores: While no one really enjoys doing household chores, looking at them as a way to practice mindfulness meditation makes them feel much less like meaningless drudgery. What's more, they will often provide you with a way to practice mindfulness while still being outwardly productive as well. When it comes to practicing mindfulness meditation in a wide variety of scenarios successfully it is essential to keep in mind that it can be done during any physical activity that doesn't require a lot of complicated mental activity.

When it is time to tackle your chores, the first thing you will want to do is go ahead and clear your mind and get in touch with the signals that your body is putting out. Once you have primed your mind, you will then want to commit yourself to the moment to moment nature of the activity you are currently taking part in and ensure that your mind doesn't just tune out the way most people allow it to while doing chores or other relatively mindless tasks. Instead, you are going to want to start by focusing on the way your hands feel as they are going through the motions of the task at hand.

Likewise, you are going to want to take in all of the information that your eyes are providing you as you go through the task, and watch as what you are doing alters the state of the physical world around you. Additionally, you are going to want to take in the smells of the task and consider what they signify. Finally, when you complete one task, take a few moments and enjoy the feeling of accomplishment that comes along with a job well done while picturing the difference in the before and after related to the task you just completed. For the best results, ensure that you prepare everything you need to do for all of your chores before you start practicing mindfulness meditation so that you can string the meditative state together for as long as possible. Once you get the hang of it, you should easily be able to sustain a mindful state for an hour or more at a time.

Bathe mindfully: It doesn't matter if you typically bathe in the morning or at night, you can always use this time to practice mindfulness as a means of helping you prepare for the day ahead or to decompress from the stress of a long day. While it is common to rush through a quick bath or shower without really thinking about it, the fact of the matter is that this time is often rife with sensations that your body is aware of, even if you are not. It is also devoid of all but the most minor distractions which means it is more or less perfect for a short burst of mindfulness meditation.

Before you begin your bathing ritual, you are going to want to take an extra few moments to center yourself and prime your mind for mindfulness while getting in touch with your body. If it is the first thing you do in the morning, make an extra effort to avoid all thoughts of the day ahead while you prepare yourself and if it is already evening then you will want to make a concentrated effort to think about the day that is coming to a close and instead work on being as in the moment as possible. Once this is done, you will want to step into the bath or shower and start by letting the feeling of the water on your skin wash over you. Consider the temperature and the way it engulfs your body completely, reaching every inch of your skin.

Use the repetitive tasks that you are performing as a gateway to reach a mental state that is free of anything but the sensations you are feeling right now. Smell is also an extremely powerful sense in this instance and focusing on the scents that surround you is also a fantastic way to push out other thoughts as they try to intrude.

Exercise mindfully: While it might not seem like it at first, the truth of the matter is that the mindset of someone who is exercising diligently is actually not all that far removed from the mindset of someone who is actively practicing mindfulness meditation. This is due to the fact that exercise automatically places bodily sensations at the forefront of the mind which is then coupled with the extreme concentration that comes along with the most productive and proactive workout routines. What all this means is that it only takes a little extra push to go from this mindset to one that is fully mindful. What's more, studies show that those who practice being mindful while exercise actually report an increased level of endurance and a general improvement to their overall performance.

The key to doing so effectively lies in changing your focus from doing every move exactly right from a mental perspective and to instead rely on letting your body take care of itself and place the focus entirely on the individual body parts that you are pushing to their limits. Consider how they feel as they move and the sensations they are providing you with as you put them through their paces. Every time you complete an exercise and move onto the next, take an extra moment to pause and refocus your attention fully on the moment and banish any other thoughts that may be trying to creep their way in.

As you focus on the moment, it is important not to do so to the extent that you lose track of what you are doing completely as doing so is a good way to accidentally push yourself past your limits and cause undue strain on the body. With that being said, it doesn't matter so much what type of exercise you choose to focus on; there are always going to be plenty of sounds, smells and sights to ensure you remain as focused on the moment as possible.

For the absolute best results, you are going to want to start with a focus on what you are doing and then let your body drop into a rhythm as you focus on the sensations all around you instead. With practice, this will allow you to easily find the sense of inner peace that you are aiming for.

Interact with social media mindfully: While it may seem surprising if you go about doing so in the right way, spending time with Facebook or Instagram can actually be a very mindful experience. While it is easy to get distracted from your goal while interacting with social media, with practice, you will find that the time you spend doing so can leave you feeling quite centered and ready to face the next challenge that awaits you.

For this type of mindfulness to be effective, the first thing you are going to want to do is to limit potential distractions as much as you can. This is crucial because most people interact with social media while multitasking which will make practicing mindfulness much more difficult. Once you have cleared the distractions out of the way, you will then want to clear your mind and focus on the moment as much as possible, once you reach the proper mindset, you will then want to look at old pictures from events that you participated in and throw the full weight of your mental energy into reliving those experiences as completely as possible.

For every picture that you look at, you will want to try and remember everything that was happening at that moment. Remember the way you felt and let it wash over you as thoroughly as possible. Put yourself back into that moment and consider the signals that your body was providing you with at the time. Once you are settled into the memory, consider the smells that go along with it as well as the physical sensations. Remember the way the temperature felt on your skin, the sounds of the memory and the things your ears were focused on whether you were actively aware of them or not. With enough practice, you will realize that you have the ability to block out virtually all the stimuli in the present day and exist solely in your memories.

CHAPTER 8: WHY IS SELF-REGULATION SO IMPORTANT?

When it comes to ensuring that your mental health is where it needs to be, it is essential to understand that it is unlikely there will ever come a time where you can completely consider the battle truly won. As such, a large part of your long-term success is going to come from self-regulation. This quality refers to the ability to stay in control of your own behavior, desires, emotions, and impulses. It means knowing how to say "no" to gratification and pleasure at the moment to reach fulfillment and satisfaction in the future, which is much more meaningful, in many cases. This ability is needed for getting past bad habits like drinking, smoking, drugs, and other addictions in addition to helping you remain in control of any mental health issues you have previously maintained to a manageable level.

While those who lack self-regulation likely think that it is an innate behavior, in all actuality it is a skill which means that like any skill it can be improved with practice over time. There are some ways that you can strengthen your resolve and improve your ability to maintain your self-regulation even when it may seem difficult or impossible to do so; first, however, you must understand that it is up to you, and no one else, to make better choices in the first place. Your future self is directly influenced by what you choose to do in the present, do yourself a favor and choose wisely.

Commit completely: When you start out down the path to self-regulation it is important to dedicate yourself to the admittedly monumental task ahead of you. Commit to the idea fully and without reservation as once you do the day to day interactions you must undertake to pursue your chosen course of action become much easier. Try making a promise on something you hold dear or even just yourself, whatever it may be; by dedicating yourself to the task at hand will make it that much easier to drown out any voices of dissension or excuses your mind might put forth to allow you an easy out from your goal. If you do not commit entirely you run the risk of giving up and returning to negative habits and losing months or even years of work.

Understand your weaknesses: Everyone has common triggers related to their mental health issues that lead to negative behaviors. When first starting out with the goal of improving your self-regulation it can be helpful to look inward and make a list of what you want to change and the items, settings or activities that trigger the negative behaviors you wish to change. While it can be difficult to confront yourself so bluntly all at once, looking at what you need to change will make it easier to establish ways to change it.

Practice makes perfect: If you feel that you will have an especially hard time deviating from a negative habit or routines, it can be helpful to try avoiding whatever it may be for a short period of time to allow yourself the opportunity to know what fully committing to a more self-regulated lifestyle will be like thus enabling you to prepare for its effects beforehand. While a practice session can be beneficial, if you let it to turn into several such sessions then you are really just prolonging the negative habit. Be frugal when determining which situations require a practice session as they can easily do more harm than good when handled carelessly.

Exercises to improve your self-regulation

Cognitive restructuring techniques: If you looked at another person's cognitive distortions you would likely find them easy to dispute. For example, no matter how much a friend of yours feels as though they are absolutely the worst, you can see why this is untrue. However, when it comes to your personal cognitive distortions, you will likely find them much more challenging to overcome which is why they persist in the first place. You will find that, without help, you will continue to believe in your own cognitive distortions no matter how they actually differ from the way the world really is.

Luckily there are several different ways to tear down your cognitive distortions, no matter how deeply held they might be. These techniques can be used at any time you find yourself coming up against a cognitive distortion and, with enough practice, you will find yourself coming up against them less and less often, and they will be replaced with balanced, accurate thoughts instead.

First, you are going to want to utilize what is known as Socratic questioning. The Greek philosopher Socrates always emphasized the importance of questions as a means of exploring otherwise complicated ideas and uncovering inherent assumptions. To make use of his method when it comes to cognitive distortions, you will want to assess that you are looking at things through their filter by asking some different questions of yourself. These questions include:
- Is this a realistic thought?
- What is the basis for the thought, is it feelings or is it facts?
- Does this thought have any evidence to back it up?
- Is it possible that I am misinterpreting the evidence

based on cognitive distortion?
- Is this situation more complicated than simply black or white?
- Is this a habitual thought or is it supported by the facts of the current situation?

While it can be easy to rush through the questions just to get them out of the way, this won't do you any good in the long run. Instead, it is best to spend a few minutes on each question to come up with an accurate answer. As you become more skilled at this exercise, you will find that you are able to accurately move through the questions more quickly. As a bonus, taking the time to think through each question will also give you time to think before you react to the scenario, decreasing negative feelings and actions that may have occurred had you not taken the time to do so.

Think about your patterns: While it can be difficult to break habits that have been formed over the years, if not decades, as ways to deal with your anxiety, a good place to start is by questioning the validity of habits that you naturally assume are beneficial to you in some way, shape or form. The easiest way to go about doing so is to just call them on their bluff.

For example, if your anxiety makes it difficult for you to take breaks while you are working under the auspices that not taking breaks makes you more efficient overall, then the easiest way to put this habit to the test is by simply measuring how long it takes for you to complete common tasks, both based on the way you are currently and an alternate schedule where you take regular breaks. Then, you would have all of the data you need to properly assess the situation, without any guesswork coming into play at all.

Even after you have gone ahead and disproven the efficacy of a particular habit, that doesn't mean that it is immediately going to disappear, far from it. This is due to the way the brain works, which is by sending the neurons that cause thoughts to become actions along the pathways in your mind that have the least resistance. The more familiar a pattern is, the less resistance its pathway is going to have. As such, to change a habit successfully, you are going to want to start by making small changes that won't represent a dramatic change to the pathway all at once.

For example, if you want to eat healthier, going from eating junk food to eating salads for every meal isn't going to stick no matter how good your intentions. Instead, you are going to want to switch to healthier products that mimic unhealthy foods first, so that the neural pathway can accept the basics of the change before leaning on it too heavily. While this is a good start towards changing your patterns for good, it is essential to keep it up once the change starts, and not partially alter the habit and call it good.

Practice silent meditation: To prepare yourself for the meditative exercise of silence meditation, you will need to start with a full run of the meditative exercise discussed in the previous chapter. You will not want to take any sort of break between the types of meditation and instead will want to go directly from one to the other. You will want to follow the same overall guidelines for both rounds of meditation, save for a few differences that will be touched on shortly. In general, you will want to retain a relaxed position and maintain a steady breathing pace. The overall process of silence meditation involves deciding on an absolute fact, personalizing that fact, deciding on what you will do with that fact, crystalizing it, negating it and then letting it go.

You will start by picking out the fact that you know to be absolutely true. Silence meditation works by manifesting the energy that you built up with the starter exercise and channeling it into awakening your kundalini and in the process granting you a deeper level of understanding the fact that supersedes traditional knowledge. Doing so will help to make it easier for you to reach the heart of the matter in ways that cannot otherwise be found without a great amount of study and dedication.

To find the fact that you will be the most successful with you will need to consider the irrefutable things that you know to be true when it comes to your current emotional or mental condition. The goal is for this description to be as accurate and irrefutable as possible, coming up with a version of the truth, not the actual truth, won't serve to accomplish much of anything.

If you are having a hard timing coming up with the right fact to use, the first thing you will want to keep in mind is that the fact should be as true as you understand anything to ever be, there is no room for wiggle room in this exercise. Next, you will want to ensure that it is important to you at this point in time. It is also important to thoroughly understand the topic, to the best of your current abilities.

The truth that you choose should be one that reflects the state of your mental and emotional state as it is currently, not in a way that you wish it were. The point of this meditative exercise is to choose a goal that can be used to gain insight right away, not when it will be eventually useful in the future. Furthermore, the fact that you ultimately decide on should be something internal, not a fact such as the earth revolving around the sun.

For example, a great starter silence meditation topic could be that desire causes most of the issues in your life. It is simple, straightforward, and could legitimately lead to real results in the near future. After you have practiced this type of meditation for a time, you will be surprised at how much simpler the world suddenly becomes.

Another question that always bears additional meditation is the inherent struggle that defines life. From the very moment we are born, life is a constant struggle in every way possible. You are always struggling against your peers for recognition and promotion, struggling to find a mate, struggling to maximize your time, the list goes on and on. While the specific results of your current struggles aren't always going to be immediately clear, having a deeper understanding of them will surely improve the quality of your life in one way or another.

To use this fact with silence mind meditation, you will first want to make sure that you understand the fact on an intellectual level which is why you will want to ensure you really understand your current struggles as much as possible. The question you will want to consider specifically is how it could be possible to free yourself from your struggles in the long-term. While the answer to this question is always going to be different, it is always going to be productive as well.

While determining if something is a fact is pretty straightforward, determining if it is the right fact can be much more difficult. To do so, you will to take a mental inventory and determine which facts you have that make you mentally recoil in terror at the thought of them. Remember, breaking new emotional or mental ground will take resolve, but if you stick with it, then it can provide you with some truly surprising breakthroughs.

Finally, don't forget to ensure that you understand what you are looking for answers about on an intellectual level. This level of understanding will then make it easier for you to determine how the fact affects all facets of your life and how you might more easily go about making the kinds of changes that will benefit you the most in both the short and the long run.

Once you truly understand the fact that you have chosen, the next thing you will want to do is personalize it in a way that is relevant for this particular meditation session. As an example, if you went with the desired fact listed above, then to personalize the fact you would then focus on times in the past when desire led you directly to additional hardship.

Once you have determined the specific tone the day's meditation will take, the next thing you will need to do is to ensure that you are ready to actually perceive the fact. While you will hopefully already understand the fact that you are contemplating, there is more to the mind than just intellect which means you will need to do more to ensure you are ready for the details on the fact you have decided upon. To do this, you will need to focus your intentions on seeing examples of the fact and nothing else. You will need to remain firm in your focus as it will be quite common for your mind to throw up other images while you are looking for relevant content. This will be especially true if you are tackling a difficult topic that it would rather not face directly.

At this point, you will likely find distractions flying at you from all sides. When this occurs, you will need to focus all of your energy on seeing the fact in action in as many different ways as possible. When doing so, you will want to try your hardest to reach back into those memories and relieve them as fully as possible. Focus on the smallest details, the sights, the sounds, the smells, and try and learn from each of them as much as possible.

The first few times that you try this meditative exercise, you are likely not going to get very far. This is perfectly normal, however, as most people often have difficulty relying on more than their analytical mind to move throughout the day to day world which means that remembering outside those guidelines can be trickier than initially anticipated. If this sounds like you then you will need to do everything in your power to ensure that you can relive the scene is as full color as you can manage. Making a habit of seeing your flaws in action should be enough to push you from merely considering the fact to actually going through with the changes that you can make regarding it as quickly as possible.

After you have broken through this mental barrier and successfully seen to the heart of the matter, the next thing you will need to do will likely happen naturally without so much as a conscious thought. Specifically, the energy that you have been building up will activate your understanding in a way you have never previously experienced, leading you to connect with a higher consciousness and thus come to understand everything about how it affects you completely without a need to dwell on it anymore. This is going to be the moment where your intelligence and attention are both at their beak, and ways to avoid constantly falling into old traps should soon be made apparent. You will not only find yourself understanding all aspects of the question with a new clarity, but life itself as well.

Once you are clear on everything that was previously unknown fact you were meditating on, the next step is the negation phase where you come to understand all of the ways in which the question was negatively affecting your life and then determines that it is better off without whatever was previously connecting it to the question in the first place. You will eventually be able to connect the questions you ask back into a larger pattern of desire and fear which in turn leads many people to a state of incompleteness that leads to nothing but dissatisfaction. Negation is turning your back on this pattern completely and making a conscious decision to seek more from life instead.

After you have fully processed everything that can be learned from the question and the negation process the next step is letting go of the things that bound you to the question in the first place. It is essential to immediately act on the clarity that you have received in the midst of your brush with a higher plane but, unless you are well-versed in the practice, the feeling won't last. It is important to make a plan as to how you are going to move forward as productively as possible if you hope for the feeling of enlightenment that you feel in the moment to translate into something truly productive..

CHAPTER 9: MENTAL HEALTH: AWARENESS IS GREAT, BUT ACTION IS ESSENTIAL

While being aware of your mental health issues is the first step towards getting rid of them once and for all, it is essential that you understand that it really is only that, the first step. After all, all the awareness in the world won't help you actually take the required steps to start improving your condition once and for all.

Set the right goals
When it comes to improving your mental health, apparently nothing is going to happen overnight. To ensure that you stick it out for the long haul, it is important to set goals to help you keep moving forward. The type of goals you set are of the upmost importance as well, as setting the wrong goals early on can be far worse than not setting any in the first place. The best goals are what are known as SMART goals. Essentially, for a goal to be smart, it needs to be achievable, specific, measurable, realistic and timely. If you can look at your goals and ensure it has each of these, then you can be relatively sure that it is going to be worth your effort as well as the time it will take to make it into a reality.

The first SMART goal that you set should be one that is at

the same time straightforward enough to more or less ensure your success while at the same time being relevant enough to your day to day life that actually succeeding will be a moment that you can easily recall in the future when success on a future goal is not nearly so assured. This way you will start forming the right type of neural pathways as soon as possible, which will then form into patterns which will eventually become habits. With this in mind, you want to start off with a goal that is, at least tangentially connected to a negative pattern surrounding an issue regarding your mental health you are looking to change. You don't need to have an exact goal in mind at this point, just the start of an idea that you can build into something larger later on. Consider the following to ensure that you are on the right track.

SMART goals are specific: The best goals are the ones that you will always be able to clearly determine where you stand in relation to the goal. The goal should then have a clearly defined fail state as well as state that will clearly let you know when you have crossed the finish line. Specific goals are also going to be much easier to chart over time as their specificity will lend to clear sub-goals that can be linked to their success or failure.

When you choose a specific goal, you are going to want to guarantee that you have a clear idea of the following details to ensure that you have chosen a goal that is truly specific enough for your needs.
• Who you will need to work with to make the goal a reality
• What you will need to do to get started on completing the goal
• Where you will need to go to see the goal through to completion
• Why you wanted to get started achieving the goal in the first place
• When you can realistically expect the goal to be achieved

- How you will go about completing the goal in various steps

SMART goals are easily measured: In addition to being specific, you want the goal that you ultimately land on to be one whose progress can easily be measured as you go along. Not only will this help you to more easily stay on track throughout the entire process, but it will also make the overall change easier to attain as it will be done in incremental pieces that you can feel good about completing every single time. This incremental process will help allow you to create the types of new neural pathways that you are looking for as they are the first step to creating the types of positive patterns that promote change that you are looking for.

When it comes to doing the actual measuring, the metric that you choose can either be one that is based on achieving specific goals or simply improving time over time, the details don't matter as long as your measurements allow you to clearly determine points for success as well as failure. If you don't have a fear of failure to help motivate you, odds are the going will seem a lot tougher than it otherwise might.

SMART goals are attainable: A good goal is one that is realistically attainable which means that you understand any potential roadblocks that may stand between you and the goal in question and that they will be ultimately surmountable. This means you are going to want to take a good hard look at your goal from all sides and be realistic with yourself about your chances for success. While looking at your goal through rose-colored glasses might make you feel better, it is truly in your best interest to be as critical during this step as possible.

Likewise, a good goal should be within the realm of possibility. All the planning and measuring in the world will never do you any good if you have decided to work towards a goal that is never going to be able to be achieved, no matter what. If the goal you are working for doesn't seem realistically attainable, you will find it much harder to focus on it with the real determination you are going to need to see any goal through to completion, making it even more unlikely you are going to be able to attain it still. Stick with goals that remain in the realm of possibility for the best results.

SMART goals are realistic: A realistic goal is one that you are both able and willing to strive for in the current climate. It doesn't matter if you would be able to accomplish the goal if another set of circumstances were true, focus on the here and now and work from there. Realistic goals are also those that are set at a level where it will require work to reach them while at the same time not requiring too much work that they seem forever out of reach. Realistic goals that require a moderate amount of effort to achieve tend to create the most motivational force.

SMART goals are time-sensitive: While a good goal contains a wide variety of important properties, one of the most important is that you include a timetable as to when the goal will be completed. Even the most specific, measurable, attainable and relevant goals will never be finished if you leave them open-ended as you will never feel the deadline closing in and begin to work harder accordingly.

It is always important to do your research and be honest with yourself when it comes to setting realistic, attainable timetables as setting an unrealistic time frame, and then not meeting it will train your brain to think that self-discipline doesn't lead to positive results. This means your mind will just be able to add additional excuses to your mind's repertoire moving forward and make it harder for you to improve your ability to practice self-discipline moving forward.

Once you have set a realistic time frame for success, the next thing you will want to do is to take a look at your goal and determine the best way to ensure you continue moving in the right direction. Like the overall goal, the benchmarks you choose to measure your success need to be reasonable otherwise instead of motivating you to success the perceived failure will give you a reason to blow off the long-term goal.

With effective benchmarks in place, it is time to start working on achieving your goal once and for all. During this process, it is important for you to focus on what you can do every day to reach your current short-term benchmark while always keeping the long-term goal in mind as well. The more tasks that you can equate to moving you towards your long-term goal the more effective and efficient you will be between now and then.

Try self-hypnosis and stop procrastinating
If, despite your best efforts, you can't seem to find the motivation you need to get started, practicing self-hypnosis might be just the ticket. When you first begin using hypnotherapy, it is important to conduct sessions for at least 20 minutes at a time. Ideally, 2 sessions per day should be the goal as the extra repetition will help the autosuggestions enter your subconscious more efficiently. After you have been using self-hypnosis for long enough that your subconscious has become accustomed to accepting autosuggestions you can generally reduce your sessions without losing efficacy.

While you are first starting self-hypnosis, it is essential to direct the hypnosis at yourself by speaking at yourself. Start by saying you will do this or you will do that. After your mind has become accustomed to the exercise, you can switch to saying I if you prefer. With that in mind here are a few additional tips to maximize the effectiveness of each self-hypnosis session

- Find a routine and stick with it: Your mind is programmed to enjoy routine, take advantage of this and ensure you practice self-hypnosis at the same time every day.
- Don't lie on your back during sessions: You need to provide your full focus to what you are listening to, not spend the time fighting off sleep.
- Have different recordings for morning and evening: Include energetic suggestions in the morning and suggestions to help you sleep at night.
- Don't worry about following along: You do not have to consciously hear what you are saying on the recording, in fact, that is rather the point. Not being able to recall what you just heard is a sign the message is making its way to your subconscious.
- Section your suggestions: Each connected sections of suggestions and affirmations is referred to as a section. Sections usually last above 5 minutes and should all be generally related to a single goal. Keep each section focused on a single task. Adding a bit of music between sections will make it easier to focus on the different specifics of each one.
- Stay motivated: The more mentally prepared you are for the task at hand the more successful you will be at it.

This script is ideal for those who feel as though they just can't get started on all the wonderful things they would like to do with their lives.

Start

You are as you have always been, ambitious, hardworking, determined and a natural leader. Persistence is a key part of your character.

<Pause>

You start each day with an empty list of accomplishments and strive to fill it as completely as possible before you go to sleep that night.

<Pause>

While your life is full of demands on your time, you are energetic and able to meet the demands head-on.

<Pause>

You are relentless when it comes to pursuing goals because you enjoy doing things that make a positive difference in your own life and the lives of others.

<Pause>

You are a positive force in the world, and your empowering nature allows you to inspire others to match your Herculean work ethic and precision perfect efficiency.

<Pause>

You are a model of personal discipline and success.

<Pause>

You manage to find time to complete all of your tasks and still have time for yourself and what is important to you.

<Pause>

You know it isn't a question of one or the other but simply of how you can do both most efficiently.

<Pause>

You have time to finish every task correctly which means you never have to worry about accomplishing everything you set your mind to.

<Pause>

Every time you listen to this recording, you will find yourself even more capable of handling your to-do list that you already are.

<Pause>

You will be able to find a time and place for everything and do so successfully.

<Pause>

You will find yourself full of energy and be able to meet new tasks head on with only the smallest breaks.

<Pause>

You have no problem breaking the most complicated tasks into achievable chunks.

<Pause>

You naturally break projects into step-by-step parts for easy completion.

<Pause>

You can see every step you need to take with every task you do with extreme precision.

<Pause>

You understand your values when it comes to completing tasks on time and correctly and you never waver on them.

<Pause>

No situation is too tough for you to bring yourself and those around you through successfully.
<Pause>

You are extremely focused and naturally alert and aware which ensures you are always prepared for whatever comes next and you always will be.

<Pause>

You are able to work through a task from start to finish while successfully blocking out all distractions.

<Pause>

Minor distractions fall away as you turn your titanic focus to the task at hand.

<Pause>

Taking a few moments after finishing each task is enough to rejuvenate you for the next. The joy of a job well done is enough to propel you on to the next.

<Pause>

You know how to balance your work life and your home life and make time for each no matter what.

<Pause>

You are a winner. You know this now as you have always known it. You can't escape it; it is a part of who you are.

<Pause>

You are talented and deserve all the good things that come your way.

<Pause>

You are the most dedicated, focused person you have ever known.

<Pause>

Personal accomplishment is important because the things you do make the world around you a better place for everyone to be.

<Pause>

When you are through listening to this recording, you will be reinvigorated in your knowledge that you will win today and every day.

<Pause>

You know this, and thus, you have the confidence of someone who knows the game is rigged in their favor.

<Pause>

Regardless of the trials you face, you know you will emerge victoriously and crush the challenges you face.

<Pause>

There is nothing you cannot use your persistence to overcome.

<Pause>

This does not mean you can become lax in your success, however.

<Pause>

Every success you find should instead serve to push you to drive yourself to even greater heights.

<Pause>

To ensure this is the case it is essential to always use your predilection for success and your go-getter mentality to continue finding things to accomplish that benefit you both personally and professionally.

<Pause>

You are the most determined and focused person who has ever lived.

<Pause>

You will never find a situation that you cannot conquer when you turn your titanic will in its direction.

<Pause>

Your self-image reflects the confident winner that you are. You can have what you desire if only you decide you want it badly enough.

<Pause>

You will never have problems getting what you want as long as you try to attain it.

<Pause>

You are very good at planning in addition to execution.

<Pause>

Once you put your mind to a task, you can determine the factors for success quickly and effectively.

<Pause>

No matter the goal, no matter the scope, no matter the odds you will always come out the victor.

<Pause>

You are having a winning attitude and that will help you choose the winning strategy no matter the task.

<Pause>

As a winner, you know that you must take responsibility for actions no matter how difficult the choice that leads to them may have been.

<Pause>

The choices you made have led you to this point, and each challenge will only lead to better rewards.

<Pause>

Your word is your bond. Saying you will do something means you will follow through regardless.

<Pause>

You will be reliable, and people will rely on you because you are a winner and winners are reliable.

<Pause>

When you start something, everyone else will count on you to finish it.

<Pause>

This is only natural because you have a history and a habit of being able to finish anything that you start regardless of the difficulty that comes with it.

<Pause>

All commitments are extremely important to you and as such you will always do everything in your power to finish all that you start.

<Pause>

You never start something tomorrow that can be started today.

<Pause>

As soon as you know you have a new task you like to finish it right away so that you have more time to relax once it is finished.

<Pause>

Your knack for crossing tasks from your to-do list means you have greater freedom in life to pursue the things you really care about.

<Pause>

With every task, you do you try and work more efficiently than the task you just finished.

<Pause>

You are efficient which means everything you try and do you finish as quickly as possible without sacrificing quality.

<Pause>

You know how to find the fastest way to finish every job, and you always take the steps required to do so.

<Pause>

You enjoy creating plans and carrying them through to completion and sticking with them no matter the difficulty.

<Pause>

Having a schedule means you know just how efficient you are which makes you happy and confident in your success.

<Pause>

When you are finished working you will have more time to do the things you want to do.

<Pause>

Anything that brings you happiness is a reward for a job well done.

<Pause>

Accomplishments should be met with rewards so reward yourself, you earned it.

<Pause>

You enjoy working hard and completing tasks above all else.

<Pause>

You are now free of the crutch of procrastination that once held you back.

CONCLUSION

Thanks for making it through to the end of Mental Health: The Ultimate Guide to Achieve Mental Toughness and Take Care of Yourself Without Seeing a Therapist, let's hope it was informative and able to provide you with all of the tools you need to achieve your goals, whatever it is that they may be. Just because you've finished this book doesn't mean there is nothing left to learn on the topic, and expanding your horizons is the only way to find the mastery you seek.

Now that you have made it to the end of this book, you hopefully have an understanding of how to get started improving your mental health, as well as a strategy or two, or three, that you are anxious to try for the first time. Before you go ahead and start giving it your all, however, it is vital that you have realistic expectations as to the level of success you should expect in the near future.

While it is entirely true that some people experience serious success right out of the gate, it is an unfortunate fact of life that they are the exception rather than the rule. What this means is that you should expect to experience something of a learning curve, especially when you are first figuring out what works for you. This is perfectly normal, however, and if you persevere, you will come out the other side better because of it. Instead of getting your hopes up to an unrealistic degree, you should think of your time spent improving your mental health as a marathon rather than a sprint which means that slow and steady will win the race every single time.

Finally, if you found this book useful in any way, a review on Amazon is always appreciated!

Printed in Great Britain
by Amazon